YOUTH BIBLE STUDY GUIDE

Church,
Prayer
and Worship

Youth Bible Study Guides

Sexuality

Following God

Image and Self-Esteem

Peer Pressure

Father God

Jesus Christ and the Holy Spirit

Sin, Forgiveness and Eternal Life

Church, Prayer and Worship

Sharing Your Faith

Tough Times

Money and Giving

Hunger, Poverty and Justice

YOUTH BIBLE STUDY GUIDE

Church, Prayer and Worship

COMPILED AND WRITTEN BY
CHIP AND HELEN KENDALL

Authentic

First published 2014 by Authentic Media Ltd
Presley Way, Crownhill, Milton Keynes, MK8 0ES.
www.authenticmedia.co.uk

British Library Cataloguing in Publication Data
A catalogue record for this book is available from the British Library

ISBN-13: 978-1-86024-635-7

Scripture quotations are taken from the Holy Bible: Easy-to-Read Version™, Anglicized.
Copyright © 2013 World Bible Translation Center, a subsidiary of Bible League International.

Extracts taken from:
Andy Flannagan, *God 360°*, Spring Harvest and Authentic, 2006
Chip Kendall, *The Mind of chipK: Enter at Your Own Risk*, Authentic, 2005
Shell Perris, *Something to Shout About Journal*, Authentic, 2007
A.W. Tozer, *Whatever Happened to Worship?* Authentic, 2007
Jenny Baker, *Transforming Prayer*, Spring Harvest and Authentic, 2004
Jenny Baker, *Vibrant Spirituality*, Spring Harvest and Authentic, 2004
Andy Frost and Jo Wells, *Freestyle*, Authentic, 2005

Cover and page design by Temple Design
Cover based on a design by Beth Ellis
Printed in Great Britain by Bell and Bain, Glasgow

Father, I pray that all who believe in me can be one. You are in me and I am in you. I pray that they can also be one in us. Then the world will believe that you sent me. I have given them the glory that you gave me. I gave them this glory so that they can be one, just as you and I are one. I will be in them, and you will be in me. So they will be completely one. Then the world will know that you sent me and that you loved them just as you loved me.

(John 17:21–23)

Chip and Helen Kendall are Creative Arts Pastors at Audacious Church, Manchester, and also love spending as much time as possible with their kids, Cole, Eden and Elliot. They currently reside in Stockport, England and they still have trouble understanding each other's accents.

Chip tours the world, fronting the Chip Kendall band. His album *Holy Freaks* and first book, *The Mind of chipK: Enter at Your Own Risk* has helped loads of young people grow in their faith. He's also the driving force behind a new youth media movement called MYvoice with Cross Rhythms, as well as being a regular presenter on GodTV. All of these jobs continue to pave the way for him to speak at events everywhere. www.chipkendall.com

After working for ten years as a dancer and tour/bookings manager, Helen now juggles looking after the kids with her work at Audacious Church helping to develop dance and all things creative. She also enjoys doing some writing and project management. Helen loves the variety in her life, and no two days are ever the same.

Guest writer, Ben Jack

Through his role as director of the resourcing organization Generation Now, and as a speaker and author, Ben is committed to helping youth and young adults question, evaluate, understand and live for a faith in Jesus. Ben is passionate about exploring narrative – particularly through film – and the role of story in our faith and lives, as well as culture, philosophy and theology. Ben is also known as award-winning DJ and producer Galactus Jack. www.ben-jack.com / www.generation-now.co.uk

Thank Yous

Massive thanks to Malcolm Down, Liz Williams and the rest of the gang at Authentic Media for giving us the opportunity to work on these study guides . . . it's been a blast. To everyone at SFC who read the books and gave us your thoughts, we appreciate the feedback. Thanks to everyone at Audacious Church for being an amazing church family. Thanks to lovely Lucy West for the fantastic photos and Lucy Wells for the typing. To everyone who talked to Chip for the 'people clips', thanks for your honesty and willingness to put up with the quirky questions. A really huge thank you to Brian and Norma Wilson for their 'hidden pearls' of wisdom. We loved your perspective on things. Finally, big thanks to all the authors whose work we have used in this book. You are an inspiration.

CONTENTS

INSTRUCTIONS

The book you're holding in your hands is a study guide. It's a compilation of extracts from lots of other books written about this subject. It might not make you the world's expert on the subject, but it should give you lots of useful information and, even better, it should give you some idea of what the Bible has to say about . . . CHURCH, PRAYER AND WORSHIP.

What is a 'reaction box'?

Throughout the book, you'll find these helpful little reaction boxes. We've added them so that you can decide for yourself what you think about what you've just read. Here's what one should look like once you've filled it in:

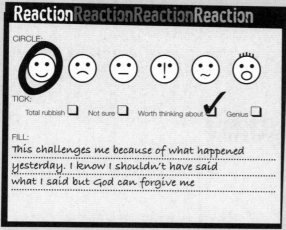

Pretty simple really . . .

Circle the face that reflects how you feel about it.

Tick the box that shows what you think about it.

Fill in any thoughts you have about what you've learned on the lines provided.

What are 'people clips'?

Just so you don't get too bored, we've added a bunch of 'people clips' to each study guide. These are people just like you, who were happy for us to pick their brains about various related topics. Who knows? Maybe you'll find someone you recognize.

What are 'hidden pearls'?

Everyone needs some good old-fashioned 'grandparently' advice, so we collected some pearls of wisdom from our friends Brian and Norma Wilson, which you can find scattered throughout the book.

What is a 'reality check'?

Finally, throughout the book you will come across sections called 'Reality check'. These should provide a chance for you to apply what you've been learning to your own life experiences.

Other than that, the only rule that applies when reading this book is that you HAVE FUN! So start reading.

Chip & Helen

Introduction

Arrive, say hello to your friends, find a seat, stand up and sing, sit down, pray, learn some stuff, talk to some more people, leave. Can you tell where we are?

Is that your experience of church or is it something different? We both attended church from a very young age. Apparently at the age of 5, Helen would always sit at the front of church on a chair next to her dad, who led worship. She would swing her legs on her seat and watch the congregation until the worship was finished. Chip grew up in a massive church in Florida with more than 2,000 people in it. His first visit was when he was one week old and he played baby Jesus in a church nativity play. Once he was a few years older he often sang songs on stage in church as part of the worship.

It is very easy just to go to church each Sunday, sing some worship songs or hymns, say some prayers and listen to a sermon without really understanding what the church is and what it is supposed to be. Whatever your experience of church is, we think **IT IS IMPORTANT TO UNDERSTAND GOD'S PLAN FOR THE CHURCH** and what is happening globally.

Is prayer just something you do once a week with your hands together and your eyes closed? Do you have to whisper and use special words? Or can it be loud and informal? Does worship always involve someone playing the guitar or organ while you stand and sing nice songs with a bunch of other people? Or can worship be honest and personal and not involve instruments at all? It is so easy to think that prayer and worship are just things we do on a Sunday morning and not during the rest of the week. In fact **PRAYER AND WORSHIP ARE SO MUCH BIGGER THAN WHAT HAPPENS AT A CHURCH MEETING** and understanding more about them could change your life and your relationship with God. This book will explore what the Bible says about church, prayer and worship, so let's get started.

All About Church

Christ loved the church and gave his life for it.

(Ephesians 5:25b)

1

First up

If you stopped 10 people in the street and asked them what church was like you would probably get 10 different answers. Churches are all different, just like Christians are all different. Some people go to church every Sunday, and others just go for Easter and Christmas. For some people church is a formal, traditional experience and for others it is like a loud, informal family party. Whether you think church is worth your regular attendance or whether you think going to church is a bit of a waste of time there is no escaping what the Bible verse on the previous page says. Take a look at it. It says that Christ gave his life for the church. He died for the church. We reckon that means that he must think that the church is pretty important.

This Life Lesson should give you an introduction to what church is. In this book we want to get you thinking about your church and how you fit into it. How important is church to you and how important are you to it? Let's start with some analysis. If you go to a church regularly, take some time to think about your place of worship and answer the questions below.

What is my church like?

....
....

How does going to church make me feel?

....
....

What do I like best about my church?

....
....

What do I like least about my church?

....
....

Church 101

Helen talks

Did you know that the Church has branches in every town in the world, more money than some whole countries, billions of members, an ever-increasing growth rate all over the globe and the ability to completely change the world? The church has more community than Facebook, more service than McDonald's and more comfort than Starbucks. Now you might be thinking, 'Hang on a minute. My church doesn't have billions of members, there are about 20 of us (10 of whom are over the age of 70!). My church never seems to have any money, let alone millions of pounds. My church isn't growing – it just lost 3 members, there's no way it can change the world!'

Whatever your personal experience of church is, you need to remember this: the church is God's plan for saving the world, it's his body here on earth right this second. Now I don't mean that by walking into a church building you are automatically a Christian. When you walk into a McDonald's you don't become a Happy Meal, right? What we mean is this: **GOD CHOSE THE CHURCH, A COMMUNITY OF BELIEVERS IN CHRIST, AS HIS WAY TO REACH, TEACH AND SERVE THE WORLD.** Church is not just a building, church is YOU. Church is groups of believers who meet together and who should be impacting their communities locally, nationally and globally.

Church is diverse, that's one of the greatest things about it. God didn't say, 'I love the church and I will give my Son for her . . . and by the way, when I say church, I mean when people come together in an old-fashioned building, sing hymns, pray and listen to a sermon.' Not at all! God didn't really set many limits on what church can be, he left that up to us. That means church can be a huge stadium in Columbia with 10,000 people shouting and praising God, or 10 old ladies in Scotland gathered in silent meditative prayer. It could be 100 believers out on the street sharing their faith, or a group of nuns in India giving out food to the poor. Church is different across the globe because people are different across the globe.

The Bible does give us some examples of what church looked like for the very first Christians in the book of Acts, so check it out. You will see that the early church shared meals, fed the poor, preached the gospel, served each other and reached out to their local community. Church isn't supposed to be a club where Christians come together and pat each other on the back for being so good for the last week, church should exist for the people outside its walls. If that isn't your experience then you need to make a difference. Don't always expect church to fix your problems – **EXPECT CHURCH TO BE THE ANSWER TO THE WORLD'S PROBLEMS**, and of course what that really means is that that means you have to get involved with answering the world's problems. OK it's a bit more challenging than turning up on a Sunday and sitting in a pew for a few hours and then going home, but take the challenge and God will work through you in a mighty way.

Hidden pearls

I think we are fortunate to be able to go to church. In other countries there are people who are in prison because they are Christians and who are isolated from other Christians. That must be very difficult. We are fortunate to be able to go to church and meet other Christians of all different ages. We feel a bit out of it sometimes, we're 40 years older than most other people, but it is good to worship as one.

Church

Bible bit

The believers shared a common purpose, and every day they spent much of their time together in the Temple area. They also ate together in their homes. They were happy to share their food and ate with joyful hearts. The believers praised God and were respected by all the people. More and more people were being saved every day, and the Lord was adding them to their group.

(Acts 2:46–47)

Shell's bit

Right . . . let's set a few things straight. So many people think that in order to be a Christian you have to go to church – what a load of rubbish! You don't *have* to go to church to be a Christian, but it is good to go to church. Let me tell you why.

I think going to church is great because it's a place where you can meet up with other people who believe the same things that you believe. It's a chance to find out more about God and learn about the Bible. You can worship and praise God. You can listen to what God's got to say to you and just enjoy being in his presence. Plus, as if that wasn't enough, you get to make lots of friends and have a cup of tea! . . . What more could you want?!

SERIOUSLY, THOUGH, GOING TO CHURCH CAN BE AMAZING – YOU JUST HAVE TO FIND THE RIGHT ONE FOR YOU.

There are loads of different types of churches: Anglican, Methodist, Baptist, Evangelical, Pentecostal, free churches . . . the list goes on. When there are so many, how do you choose a church that's right for you? Well . . . it depends what you're into.

There are different types of churches to suit different types of people. For example, some churches are big and some are really small. Some churches are loud and lively and some tend to be a little quieter. Some churches focus more on worship than others. Some churches have wooden pews and some have chairs. Some churches have a traditional way of doing things and some like to be a bit more modern. Some churches are very creative and some are more evangelistic. Again . . . the list of comparisons goes on and on.

Church doesn't have to be boring . . . all you have to do is find one that's right for you.

Time to think and pray

What do you think about going to church? Do you attend church regularly? If you're already part of a church, what do you like about it and what don't you like about it? In your opinion, what would your ideal church be like? How do you think you could get more involved in your church?

Shell Perris, *Something to Shout About Journal*, Authentic Media, 2007

ReactionReactionReactionReaction

CIRCLE:

😊 ☹️ 😐 😮 😕 😲

TICK:

Total rubbish ☐   Not sure ☐   Worth thinking about ☐   Genius ☐

FILL:

....

....

....

....

No Longer a STRANGER

Chip talks

Danny was the kind of guy who spent a lot of time on his own. He could never figure out why his friends at school seemed to act one way when they were in a group, and a completely different way when they were alone. He knew that there were always pressures to try and 'fit in' with what everyone else was doing at the time, but none of those things ever really held enough attraction for Danny to actually want to join in. So he'd just find an excuse to leave, and that was that.

There was one problem though. Danny was never genuinely satisfied when he was on his own. He felt deep down that there was somewhere out there – a place where he belonged. A place where he could be himself and still find acceptance. A place where his opinions mattered and he could contribute to something bigger than himself.

One Sunday, Danny's mum announced that she was going to church, and asked if he would like to join her. Since he couldn't think of a good enough excuse not to, Danny quickly got ready and jumped into the car. **WHEN THEY ARRIVED, HE WAS IMPRESSED WITH THE WELCOME HE RECEIVED.** There were people with shirts that read 'Here to Help' and smiles on their faces, who seemed more than happy getting stuck in with all the volunteer-type services required. Some of them were in the car park directing traffic, some of them were serving coffee, and many of them were just standing near doorways chatting to people and helping to point them in the direction of whatever they were looking for.

Danny enjoyed the party-like atmosphere during the praise and worship. He joined in with the singing and jumping once he'd relaxed a little. Then the guy who got up to preach had him in stitches within the first few minutes of his sermon. This wasn't at all what he'd expected church to be like, but Danny was having a really great time. Afterwards a few young people of about his age came up to him and introduced themselves. It didn't feel intrusive at all, and somehow Danny found himself opening up to these church kids. They didn't seem like strangers. In fact, if Danny was really honest, he felt as if he'd finally come home.

The next Sunday, Danny went to church again. This time when the leader gave an invitation to follow Jesus at the end of the service, **DANNY WENT FORWARD TO BECOME A CHRISTIAN.** Within a few months, he was volunteering to be a part of that same welcome team, the one that had captured his attention in the first place. As far as Danny was concerned, he didn't need to look any further for a place to belong. This was it.

In the Bible, we see that the early Church was a close-knit community. What are some of the characteristics of church that we find in this passage?

Acts 2:42–47

....

....

....

Are there any service teams in your church that you are already involved with? If so, list them here. If not, which would you be interested in joining?

....

....

....

Is there anything that you feel your church should be doing in order to create a better atmosphere where people feel like they belong?

....

....

....

NO COMPROMISE!

Many people's perceptions of Christianity emerge from their experiences in church meetings. I can remember that in my teen years I was excited about the stuff that happened in the Bible but couldn't get my head around the fact that church seemed so different. Some churches were about people singing stuffy hymns and listening to an old person talk in monotone, others were about singing happy songs, clapping and patting themselves on the back – they seemed to have nothing in common with the rescue mission of the Bible. Surely church wasn't meant to be so inward focused?

In the book of Acts, the church is full of action – people were joining the disciples every day and they were seeing awesome stuff happen. At the same time they were being persecuted. The message that they preached was controversial and the establishment didn't like it. They spoke of Jesus as being their Lord, not the Roman emperor. What exciting times! But how did the church get from being this cutting-edge body of revolutionary people to what it looks like today?

I BELIEVE THAT MUCH OF THE PROBLEM CAN BE SUMMED UP IN ONE WORD – *COMPROMISE*. Throughout time Christians have compromised the gospel. The gospel is the most radical message ever – God allowed his Son to die in your place and in mine. It turns the world upside down. It is a message that calls for repentance and transformation. It is a message that blows away our understanding of the world and allows us to see another dimension. It is a message that has more martyrs than any other cause. It is the message that divides history between 'before Christ' and 'after'. But it is a message that Christians continue to water down with the things of this world. Time and time again, people become complacent about their relationship with God and content with the state of the world. They sacrifice relationship for stale religion – the ultimate compromise.

The story continues across the centuries. Throughout time people have tried to make following Jesus a life based on keeping laws and joining institutions – turning the church into a lukewarm establishment rather than a powerful movement. In the eighteenth century the Church of England had become very stale – run by the rich gentry rather than those passionate for Jesus. God called John Wesley to shake it up. Though he was an Anglican vicar, he was frequently banned from preaching from the lectern and preached instead from tombstones in graveyards, on hillsides or even on his horse! He preached Jesus and saw the church become a movement once again.

IT IS TIME FOR A NEW GENERATION OF MEN AND WOMEN TO WAKE UP. I believe that God is calling revolutionaries to bring the church out of religiosity. I believe he is calling people to start putting Jesus at the centre. I believe he is calling people to start taking the gospel seriously and to start caring for the marginalized and the oppressed. I believe he is calling people out of ritual and back into relationship.

Andy Frost and Jo Wells, *Freestyle*, Authentic Media, 2005

ReactionReactionReactionReaction

CIRCLE:

TICK:

Total rubbish ☐   Not sure ☐   Worth thinking about ☐   Genius ☐

FILL:

....

....

....

....

Name: **Ross Maynard**

Age: **19**

Town: **Salisbury**

Occupation: **Lifeguard at Tidworth Leisure Centre**

Passions: **Rugby, God**

Most exquisite country you've been to?

Cyprus. My dad's a padre in the military.

Last dream you can remember?

I'm in a moving car, and I don't see anyone driving, so I climb in the front and start driving.

Person in politics you most admire/respect/look up to?

Martin Luther King Jr.

Happiest thought?

Being in God's presence.

Earliest experience of church?

When I was 8, I officially gave my life to Christ and I talked to my dad about it. But I've been going to church since the day I was born – literally!

What is at the core of worship?

It is an expression of my love for God.

Church on the Street

A while ago, when I was in thebandwithnoname, we did a gig in York Minster. We had a great time and even had the amazing privilege of meeting the Archbishop of York. I'll never forget the immensity of that ancient church. Our music seemed to reverberate for an eternity as the track echoed past the stained glass windows and up into those gothic high ceilings. Quite a sound.

The very next day we did an outdoor concert in Birmingham. Just like the York Minster gig, this one was attended by hundreds of young Christians, all of them praising God with us. Only this time, instead of being cooped up inside an ancient church, we were right out on the streets, just outside what looked like the town hall. As I gazed at the crowd among the urban high-rise buildings, I couldn't help but think that actually this was a much better representation of what the early church must've been like and, indeed, what church today should look like. A massive group of people were enjoying God right out in the open air, while unbelievers and passers-by stared at them, wondering what in the world was going on.

THE CHURCH IS NOT A BUILDING . . . IT'S THE PEOPLE INSIDE. When Jesus talked about the church he used the illustration of salt bringing out the flavour in food. He also used the example of a lamp on a lampstand.

Let's be the salt and light we're meant to be, flavouring and illuminating the outside world with a message of repentance (turning away from our old sinful lifestyles), grace (accepting the amazing free gift of God's forgiveness) and freedom (living a life totally liberated to do what God wants us to do).

God's mind

'So I tell you, you are Peter. And I will build my church on this rock. The power of death will not be able to defeat my church.'
(Matthew 16:18)

One of the men sitting at the table with Jesus heard these things. The man said to him, 'It will be a great blessing for anyone to eat a meal in God's kingdom!' Jesus said to him, 'A man gave a big dinner. He invited many people. When it was time to eat, he sent his servant to tell the guests, "Come. The food is ready." But all the guests said they could not come. Each one made an excuse. The first one said, "I have just bought a field, so I must go and look at it. Please excuse me." Another man said, "I have just bought five pairs of work animals; I must go and try them out. Please excuse me." A third man said, "I just got married; I can't come." So the servant returned and told his master what had happened. The master was angry. He said, "Hurry! Go into the streets and alleys of the town. Bring me the poor, the paralysed, the blind and the lame." Later, the servant said to him, "Master, I did what you told me to do, but we still have places for more people." The master said to the servant, "Go out to the main roads and country lanes. Tell the people there to come. I want my house to be full! None of those people I invited first will get to eat any of this food."'
(Luke 14:15–24)

Praise God in the great assembly. Praise him when the older leaders meet together.
(Psalm 107:32)

'You are as needed as salt for those on earth. But if the salt loses its taste, it cannot be made salty again. And then it is good for nothing except to be thrown out for people to walk on. You are the light that shines for the world to see. You are like a city built on a hill that cannot be hidden. People don't hide a lamp under a bowl. They put it on a lampstand. Then the light shines for everyone in the house. In the same way, you should be a light for other people. Live so that they will see the good things you do and praise your Father in heaven.'
(Matthew 5:13–16)

Your mind

- **What is my most memorable representation of what church should be like?**

  ....
  ....

- **How can I shine the 'light' God has placed in me today?**

  ....
  ....

- **Why does Jesus compare Christians to 'salt'?**

  ....
  ....

- **How can I be like 'salt' to the people around me?**

  ....
  ....

Chip Kendall, *The Mind of chipK: Enter at Your Own Risk*, Authentic Media, 2005

Reaction ReactionReactionReaction

CIRCLE:

😊 ☹️ 😐 😯 😕 😲

TICK:

Total rubbish ☐   Not sure ☐   Worth thinking about ☐   Genius ☐

FILL:

....
....
....
....

Your Part in the Church

In your life together, think the way Christ Jesus thought. He was like God in every way, but he did not think that his being equal with God was something to use for his own benefit. Instead, he gave up everything, even his place with God. He accepted the role of a servant, appearing in human form.

(Philippians 2:5–7)

First up

Let's be honest, most churches have some funny people in them. You know, the guy at the back with the 1960s-patterned, knitted sweater that he has been wearing every Sunday for the last 4 years; the old lady who insists on giving you a big kiss every time you walk in the door; the small child who always insists on wiping their snotty nose on your leg and calling you Dada.

Sometimes it can be hard to fit into church as a young person. Many churches don't have lots of other young people and it can feel like you don't really have a place, or anything to give. We think that local church is really important and that as a young person you should be playing a huge part in your church, you should be leading the way and keeping all the older people on their toes. We also believe that the best way to get involved in your church and to change it for the better is to serve. Do what Jesus did and serve others, no matter what they look like, or how different they are from you.

We asked Rob, the leader of Stockport Family Church, what he would like to see young people in the church doing. This is what he said: 'Get involved with any "church stuff" you can: perform, create some music, do a reading, drama, a poem, make some art or animation for the church, write an article, give a testimony, preach a mini-sermon, help with stewarding, PA, serving drinks, clearing up/setting out, helping with younger ones, helping with older ones, suggest new ideas and, of course, don't eat all the biscuits!' Many church leaders and church members are desperate for young people to get involved and make their mark on the church.

In the last Life Lesson we looked at the church generally, but now we want you to think about the part you can play in the church. Answer the questions below to get you started.

Go back to Life Lesson 1 (p.14) and read what you wrote for the things you like least about your church. How could you change these things and make them better?

....

....

Think of something you could do on a Sunday morning to serve your church. Write it down and then commit to doing it.

....

....

Servanthood

chipK's mind

One of the toughest things to maintain when I'm out on the road with my band is an attitude of service. I'm constantly reminding myself that I'm there to serve – not just the organizers of the event, but also my fellow band members and even the people who are just there to enjoy the show. There are many examples in the Bible of what it means to be a servant – heroes like Joseph, Daniel, Ruth and Onesimus. Jesus can be seen washing his disciples' feet, a job usually done by the household slave of the time. But I'd like to tell you about a modern-day servant-hero who I've come across in my travels. His name is Charles.

Charles is a retired solicitor who lives in Tunbridge Wells, UK. He has a lovely wife, grown-up kids, a very nice big house and a posh English accent. He's extremely 'well read' and at the end of every conversation I have with him, I always feel smarter than I did before. **BUT THE COOLEST THING I'VE LEARNED ABOUT CHARLES IS HIS WILLINGNESS TO SERVE.** He's always been a tuxedo-wearing steward at the gigs we've done in the area, helping out wherever he is needed the most. And at the last GrassRootz festival we played, he was found picking up litter all over the muddy campsite. Just picture, a posh, retired solicitor bent over, scooping up dirty, wet rubbish! That's what I want to be like. That's what Jesus asks all of us to be like. That's what I call a servant.

God's mind

So Jesus called the followers together. He said, 'You know that the rulers of the non-Jewish people love to show their power over the people. And their important leaders love to use all their authority over the people. But it should not be that way with you. Whoever wants to be your leader must be your servant. Whoever wants to be first must serve the rest of you like a slave. Do as I did: the Son of Man did not come for people to serve him. He came to serve others and to give his life to save many people.'
(Matthew 20:25–28)

Jesus' followers began to have an argument about which one of them was the greatest. Jesus knew what they were thinking, so he took a little child and stood the child beside him. Then he said to the followers, 'When you accept a little child like this as one who belongs to me, you accept me. And anyone who accepts me also accepts the one who sent me. The one among you who is the most humble – this is the one who is great.'
(Luke 9:46–48)

When Jesus had finished washing their feet, he put on his clothes and went back to the table. He asked, 'Do you understand what I have just done for you? You call me "Teacher". And you call me "Lord". And this is right, because that is what I am. I am your Lord and Teacher. But I washed your feet like a servant. So you also should wash each other's feet. I did this as an example for you. So you should serve each other just as I served you. Believe me, servants are not greater than their master. Those who are sent to do something are not greater than the one who sent them. If you know these things, great blessings will be yours if you do them.'
(John 13:12–17)

Whoever has the gift of serving should serve.
(Romans 12:7a)

Your mind

- **Who has God called me to serve?**

....

....

- **Where are my services needed the most?**

....

....

- **Who do I know who's a real servant?**

....

....

- **I will serve those around me today by:**

....

....

Chip Kendall, *The Mind of chipK: Enter at Your Own Risk*, Authentic Media, 2005

ReactionReactionReactionReaction

CIRCLE:

TICK:

Total rubbish ☐   Not sure ☐   Worth thinking about ☐   Genius ☐

FILL:

....

....

....

....

Teamwork

Helen talks

As part of my job at Innervation Trust I often interviewed people who wanted jobs in bands or teams that we were setting up. I'd always ask them how they felt about working in a team, as that is a huge part of the day-to-day life of a band. Every single person I have ever asked that question has always said something like, 'Oh I love teamwork and I work well in a team with other people.' Most of them went on to explain that they prefer working in a team to working alone and that they would enjoy that side of the job. Sounds good right? The only thing is that once these people started working in our teams, about 90% of them would come to me at some point or another because they had problems with the other members of their team! All the people who told me they loved teamwork and working with other people realized that, although it sounds very nice and fuzzy, it's not all that much fun having to deal with other people. But you know what, the ones who have stuck at it and worked hard at fixing and building relationships have come out changed as people, and with friendships that will last a lifetime.

t can be a bit like that being part of God's ultimate team, the church. The Bible says this about it:

A person has only one body, but it has many parts. Yes, there are many parts, but all those parts are still just one body. Christ is like that too. Some of us are Jews and some of us are not; some of us are slaves and some of us are free. But we were all baptized to become one body through one Spirit. And we were all given the one Spirit.

(1 Corinthians 12:12–13)

Basically what Paul, the writer of 1 Corinthians, is saying is that we may all be different on the outside, but we are all part of Christ's body. We are God's representation on earth with a mission to demonstrate who he is to the world. Now that is all good; the difficult part comes with that little word 'different'.

Other people in your church may be different to you; they may do things that you think are silly or boring or irrelevant. Have you ever stopped to think that they might be an 'eye' and you might be a 'hand'? To an eye, what the hand does may seem ridiculous, all that moving around, jumping about grabbing at things! An eye would never behave in such a way. But without the differences between the eye and the hand you would have an incomplete body.

One of the hardest things about teamwork is **LEARNING TO APPRECIATE THE DIFFERENCES** between you and your team members, instead of trying to change everyone to be like you! As the church, God's body, we have an amazing opportunity to rub shoulders with people we normally wouldn't, to show love to people we might normally not come into contact with. To people outside the church that is an attractive thing. Jesus said this about getting along with the rest of the body:

'I give you a new command: love each other. You must love each other just as I loved you. All people will know that you are my followers if you love each other.'

(John 13:34–35)

If we want to fulfil our mission as the body of Christ we need to love each other – and that includes other churches, other youth groups and other ministries too. We are one body and Christ is the head, let's start appreciating all the different parts we couldn't live without.

ReactionReactionReactionReaction

CIRCLE:

TICK:

Total rubbish ☐ Not sure ☐ Worth thinking about ☐ Genius ☐

FILL:

....

....

....

....

Name: **Emily Partridge**

Age: **16**

Town: **Andover**

School subjects: **Music, Photography**

What do you want to be when you grow up?

I have no idea. Whatever God wants.

Do you have any siblings?

Three brothers. It's annoying when they stand in front of the telly when I'm trying to watch.

What's the biggest difference between your Christian friends and the non-Christian ones?

I don't have that many non-Christian friends, but the ones I have are into sex and alcohol – not to sound too clichéd. They're not as funny.

Do you ever pray with your brothers?

No. Maybe once when I was putting them to bed. That's it.

Do you ever pray with your parents?

Yes.

Is it awkward?

Not really. My dad's the worship leader and the youth leader, so it's quite natural.

Chip talks

This was not turning out to be a great day for Charlotte. It was only lunchtime, and already she'd managed to:

- **Accidentally sleep in**
- **Spill milk on her school uniform**
- **Completely zone out during an important science lesson**
- **Embarrass herself in front of the guy of her dreams**
- **And really upset Laura, her best friend**

When would something finally start to go right?

Thankfully, after school finished Charlotte was able to walk all the way home without a hitch. As soon as she got back to her room, she burst into tears and collapsed onto her bed. Her emotions just couldn't be bottled up any longer. She stayed there for a long time, replaying the worst moments of the day over and over in her mind. What was she going to say to Laura? How could she ever face seeing or being seen by 'you-know-who' ever again?

At dinner, Charlotte's mum asked her if she wanted to join her for Life Group later that night. It was just a small group of people from their church that got together regularly to pray for each other and talk about what God was doing in their lives.

'I DON'T KNOW, MUM. I'VE HAD A PRETTY ROUGH DAY TODAY. I DON'T REALLY FEEL LIKE IT. I'D RATHER JUST STAY AT HOME.'

But after a few minutes, Charlotte's mum managed to convince her to tag along. The mention of free cookies and cake helped a lot.

Life Group turned out to be exactly what Charlotte needed. Everyone was very easy-going and when she was casually asked if there was anything she wanted prayer for, Charlotte felt safe enough to say yes. She opened up about what had happened that day, and afterwards she genuinely felt loads better. When the praying had finished, a few people hung around a little longer, chatting to each other. One lovely elderly lady struck up a conversation with Charlotte and actually had some pretty sound advice for her. Maybe this wasn't going to end up being such a bad day after all.

God designed church to be a fully functioning family. No one's perfect, and everyone needs one another in order to get through life – the good parts and the not so good parts. Read Romans 12:4–16, and answer the following questions:

- **How does this passage reflect Charlotte's experience?**
- **When was the last time I really opened up to someone?**
- **What advice have I been given by someone who genuinely cares?**
- **What are some of the benefits of being part of a Life Group?**

ReactionReactionReactionReaction

CIRCLE:

TICK:

Total rubbish ☐   Not sure ☐   Worth thinking about ☐   Genius ☐

FILL:

....

....

Hidden pearls

I think it's wonderful to have young people in the church. We are very blessed to have young people in our church. I like their enthusiasm and their love of the Lord. They've got much more ability to do things for him. When I hear of the activities they are doing I think it's wonderful.

Take Some Time to GOSSIP WITH A GRANNY

Helen talks

Are there any old people in your church? Do you ever talk to them? Do you think they have personalities and things to say, or do you just lump them all together as 'old people'? Recently I went to a pub for Sunday dinner and I noticed a young family joined by an elderly relative. While the parents were taking great care to make sure that Granny was comfortable and involved in conversation, the youngest member of the family, a 10-year-old boy, seemed totally absorbed in his PSP games console and totally unabsorbed in Granny. I was struck by how he was missing out on a great opportunity. The old lady at the table would probably only be a part of his life for maybe another 5 or at most 10 years, but instead of asking questions, learning about an era of life that he would never experience, and perhaps gaining some insight, he was too preoccupied with his game.

H ave you ever noticed that we live in a world where the old are often ignored, silenced and sidelined. Think about it. When was the last time you saw anyone over 70 on TV being interviewed about something not directly related to the elderly? When did you last read a magazine or web article written for a mainstream audience by someone over 70? Most media forms encourage the idea that the old have nothing of relevance to say to the rest of us. I think we are missing out. We are often in such a hurry that we can't be bothered to take the time to talk to old people; it's quicker to find out what we need to know on the Internet.

One of the great things about belonging to a church is that usually there is a mix of people from all different age groups and walks of life. As a Christian you may get more of an opportunity to spend time with old people than some of your non-Christian friends do. So take some time to talk to them. Many older people have had influential careers in their time or have brought up families or been through wars and other hardships that we can only imagine. **THEY ALL HAVE AN AMAZING PERSPECTIVE ON LIFE THAT I GUESS ONLY LIVING A LONG TIME CAN GIVE YOU**. Many old people are lonely and would just love to chat, and spending time with them is a great way for you to serve your church. So go somewhere quiet, take a short stroll, go for a visit and make them a cup of tea, get some shopping for them and make sure you really listen while they talk. Ask questions, learn secrets. Because if not now then when? They don't have forever, and the next generation of older people will not have experienced the things that these have. You might learn something new.

ReactionReactionReactionReaction

CIRCLE:

TICK:

Total rubbish ☐   Not sure ☐   Worth thinking about ☐   Genius ☐

FILL:

....

....

....

....

The Fingerprints of God

Ben Talks

Stop motion animation (SMA) is a painstaking process. To produce moving images, the animators photograph objects – often, but not exclusively, clay models – over and over, moving them slightly each time. Every second of film is, traditionally, made from 24 individual images (frames), which when played back create the illusion of movement that the eye perceives. So, to produce just ten minutes of film, you need to produce 14,400 images!

To create a feature-length stop motion animated film, you are going to need the involvement of a number of people with various skill sets. Scriptwriters, storyboard artists, model makers, a cinematographer, editor, composer, people working on continuity, sound design, props, effects, set design and of course, most importantly of all, catering. This list only skims the surface of all the people that may be involved in the process, each person playing a crucial role in creating a cinematic masterpiece.

Something quite unique to the use of clay models in SMA is that you can sometimes see where the animator has left an imprint in the clay. This can be, quite literally, the fingerprint of the creator on the creation.

God is looking for his people to use all of the different skills, gifts and personalities that he gives us, to become a beautiful church which has the clear, identifiable fingerprints of the creator God all over it. Let's celebrate our diversity, and see how God uses it to create his masterpiece!

Read 1 Corinthians 12:12–27. See also Genesis 1:27, Acts 20:28, Romans 12:4–8.

Reflect

- *What does Paul mean by many parts making one body in the verses from 1 Corinthians 12 and Romans 12?*

  - *How can we learn to use our skills to the best of our ability in church community, encourage others to do the same, and embrace the diversity of God's creation?*

Respond

- *Offer to serve your church community in the areas where they have need. As you grow in service, see how God develops your gifts and opens up new and specific areas in which to use them.*

Remember

- *Embracing God's diverse creation will lead to a church body that can meet the diverse needs of this world, and will see people using the skills and talents that God has given them for his glory.*

ReactionReactionReactionReaction

CIRCLE:

TICK:

Total rubbish ☐   Not sure ☐   Worth thinking about ☐   Genius ☐

FILL:

....

....

....

....

REALITY CHECK

DESIGN YOUR OWN CHURCH

Here's your chance to let your creativity run wild as you create your dream church. Just for fun, forget all practicalities and think up the kind of place that would help you connect with God, that would reach out to non-Christians and that would fulfil the guidelines the Bible sets out about church. Check out the verses below first:

> Many wonders and miraculous signs were happening through the apostles, and everyone felt great respect for God. All the believers stayed together and shared everything. They sold their land and the things they owned. Then they divided the money and gave it to those who needed it. The believers shared a common purpose, and every day they spent much of their time together in the Temple area. They also ate together in their homes. They were happy to share their food and ate with joyful hearts. The believers praised God and were respected by all the people. More and more people were being saved every day, and the Lord was adding them to their group.

(Acts 2:43–47)

> So, brothers and sisters, what should you do? When you meet together, one person has a song, another has a teaching and another has a new truth from God. One person speaks in a different language, and another interprets that language. The purpose of whatever you do should be to help everyone grow stronger in faith.

(1 Corinthians 14:26)

What is the name of your dream church?

Describe or draw the place where you meet.

Describe what happens when you get together with your church (activities, programme).

Describe the people in your dream church.

Write down any other details about your dream church.

Look back over what you've done. Are there any things in your dream church that you could make a reality in your real church?

GO FOR IT AND MAKE A DIFFERENCE!

All about Prayer and Fasting

Always be full of joy. Never stop praying.

Whatever happens, always be thankful.

This is how God wants you to live in Christ Jesus.

(1 Thessalonians 5:16–18)

First Up

You're sitting comfortably, watching the in-flight movie, sipping an iced Coke and nibbling your way through a tiny bag of pretzels when, BOOM, you hear an explosion towards the back of the plane. There is an eerie moment of stillness and then the cabin lights flicker and go off, plunging you into darkness. Through the frenzied beating of your heart you feel the nose of the plane start to tilt forwards and then, like something out of a disaster movie, you and the 265 other passengers on board begin plummeting towards the earth.

Is this what it would take to get you praying? It's amazing how many atheists and agnostics in moments of dire need would start to pray. They would plead with a God whose existence they had never previously acknowledged to help them, to fix the plane. They would ask for forgiveness for their sins and pray for entrance to heaven and maybe even for their loved ones back home.

We believe that prayer isn't for emergency use only! Prayer should be used every day, or as the verse on the previous page says, 'never stop praying'. Talk to God about everyday stuff: how you feel, what your fears and triumphs are, what you need, thank him for what you have, and ask him to work in the lives of others too. We hope this next Life Lesson will get you off to a good start.

What is PRAYER?

Perhaps a good place to start is to remind ourselves just what prayer is.

- **Prayer is communicating with a Father who loves us, standing alongside our brother Jesus who prays with us.**

- **Prayer is the discovery of our rightful place, creating in us a wonderful sense of homecoming and belonging.**

- **Prayer is the relief of bringing the concerns and worries that weigh us down to the God who can deal with them.**

- **Prayer is the privilege of being involved in God's story of redemption, expecting and waiting for God to change events and change us.**

- **Prayer is a paradox: it is both a place of safety, where we are most accepted and loved, and a place of risk, of God pushing us out of our comfort zone into new things.**

- **Prayer is the loneliest, most desolate place at times, where the deepest and most distressing cries of the human heart are heard.**

- **Prayer is a creative adventure – there is no formula or guarantee of 'success'.**

We are creative communicators but often our prayer follows a formula.

Think for a moment of someone you love – your mum or dad, your girlfriend or boyfriend. How would you communicate your love to that person without words? You might buy them a gift, write them a note, cook their favourite meal, clean their car for them, run them a scented, candlelit bath – I'm sure you can think of lots more ways. We are creative people who communicate with each other in many different ways and yet when we pray we follow the 'hands together, eyes closed' formula.

Like Pavlov's dog, we have a conditioned response to the phrase 'Let's pray'! We tend to shut down all the creativity that we use so effortlessly in the rest of our lives. There is something beautiful about stillness, about centring on God and being quiet. **BUT WHY IN PRAYER DO WE SHUT DOWN AND RESTRICT OUR MEANS OF EXPRESSION INSTEAD OF USING OUR GOD-GIVEN CREATIVITY AND TALENT?**

Reducing prayer to a formula sends out the message that prayer has a code of conduct, that you mustn't get it wrong. Instead of focusing on our relationship with God, we are focusing on what we are doing and whether we are getting it right. Are we using the right language? Have we gone on for long enough? Are we just repeating what someone else said? Have we missed anything out?

The other message that we pick up from the 'hands together, eyes closed' formula is that when we pray, we shut out the rest of the world. There is some wisdom in that – it's good to stop distractions and focus on God. But we also need to be able to bring the reality of our world to God in prayer. Instead of prayer being a place where we become super-spiritual in order to impress God, prayer should be a place where we bring our frail and vulnerable selves in order to become more like Jesus.

Jenny Baker, *Transforming Prayer*, Spring Harvest Publishing and Authentic Media, 2004

ReactionReactionReactionReaction

CIRCLE:

TICK:

Total rubbish ☐   Not sure ☐   Worth thinking about ☐   Genius ☐

FILL:

....

....

....

....

Prayer

Bible bit

'When you pray, don't be like the hypocrites. They love to stand in the synagogues and on the street corners and pray loudly. They want people to see them. The truth is, that's all the reward they will get. But when you pray, you should go into your room and close the door. Then pray to your Father. He is there in that private place. He can see what is done in private, and he will reward you. And when you pray, don't be like the people who don't know God. They say the same things again and again. They think that if they say it enough, their god will hear them. Don't be like them. Your Father knows what you need before you ask him. So this is how you should pray:

'"Our Father in heaven, we pray that your name will always be kept holy. We pray that your kingdom will come – that what you want will be done here on earth, the same as in heaven. Give us the food we need for today. Forgive our sins, just as we have forgiven those who did wrong to us. Don't let us be tempted, but save us from the Evil One."'

'Yes, if you forgive others for the wrongs they do to you, your Father in heaven will also forgive your wrongs. But if you don't forgive others, then your Father in heaven will not forgive the wrongs you do.'

(Matthew 6:5–15)

Shell's bit

When we live in a world that is as busy as the world we live in today, prayer can often get pushed to the bottom of our 'to do' list without us even realizing it. After all, we have to think about things like friends, family, school/work, daily responsibilities, hobbies, 'me' time . . . the list goes on.

Over the last few years I have made a discovery . . . life doesn't work when you don't make time for prayer. People have told me time and time again about the importance of prayer but it was just a bunch of words until I really understood what it meant for me personally.

I used to think that in order to pray successfully you had to set aside a certain length of time every day and just go for it. You can do that if you want to, but the best thing about praying is that you don't have to close your eyes and put your hands together . . . you can do it any time, anywhere.

I tend to do a lot of praying in the car when I'm travelling from one place to another. It's great! I'm on my own with time to spare and nothing to do but drive and pray. I do get some funny looks, though, when I stop at traffic lights and I appear to be talking to myself! I pray when I'm walking my dog and I pray sometimes when I'm cooking dinner. **PRAYER DOESN'T HAVE TO JUST HAPPEN WHEN YOU GO TO BED AT NIGHT.** I have tried praying at night before I go to sleep but it just doesn't work for me . . . I end up falling asleep.

Prayer is all about you and God communicating with each other. Look at it as though it was a mobile phone conversation. You can talk on your mobile whenever you want to. You can call other people and other people can call you. It's exactly the same when it comes to prayer.

Time to think and pray

Have a think about what times during the day you can pray. It doesn't have to be for an hour – it can be for 2 minutes if you want. Do you think prayer is important? Ask God to help you understand the importance and power of prayer. Try thinking of it like a mobile phone conversation and see if it helps.

Shell Perris, *Something to Shout About Journal*, Authentic Media, 2007

ReactionReactionReactionReaction

CIRCLE:

TICK:

Total rubbish ☐   Not sure ☐   Worth thinking about ☐   Genius ☐

FILL:

....

....

DIFFERENT TYPES OF PRAYER

There are lots of different types of prayer and it can be quite difficult to define them. Often we will move from praising God, to asking him for something, to confessing something we have done wrong without even thinking about it. Different types of prayer will overlap and flow into each other and don't need to be too strictly analysed. But for the purpose of this book, these are the definitions I have worked with:

PRAISE – looking at who God is and giving him praise.

THANKFULNESS – looking at what God has done for us and thanking him for it.

CONFESSION – telling God about where we have failed him, the sins we have committed, and asking for his forgiveness.

INTERCESSION – specifically praying on behalf of other people – standing in the gap and bringing people that we care for to God.

PETITION – asking God to do something for us or for others.

TRANSFORMATION – prayer that results in us being changed, such as promising God that we will do something, committing ourselves to his service, letting go of the things that trouble us, forgiving others.

PRAYER OF DESOLATION – a cry of despair from the heart, honest, real prayer that has nowhere else to turn but God.

BLESSING – speaking words of God's blessing to people.

CONTEMPLATION – the more meditative, silent forms of prayer, listening to God.

The categories of prayer that I have suggested alongside each idea or encounter shouldn't be seen as restrictive; most of them can be adapted to fit other types of prayer.

Jenny Baker, *Transforming Prayer*, Spring Harvest Publishing and Authentic Media, 2004

ReactionReactionReactionReaction

CIRCLE:

TICK:

Total rubbish ☐   Not sure ☐   Worth thinking about ☐   Genius ☐

FILL:

....

....

....

....

....

....

Phone Home

Don't you just hate it when your mobile phone runs out of charge? Your best friend was just about to tell you the best part of the story, and now you've got to wait until you can recharge it to call them back.

W ell, what if I was to tell you about a phone that never runs out of charge, costs absolutely nothing for both peak and off-peak minutes and, best of all, it still works even in places where there's no network coverage! You'd stand in line for hours to get your hands on one of those babies, wouldn't you? Prayer is a lot like this miracle phone. It allows us free access to the throne room of God himself, and it's available 24-7, no matter where we're 'calling' from. **GOD WANTS US TO TALK TO HIM JUST THE WAY WE ARE.** No big fancy words, no poetic rhymes, no tremendous reports on how we solved the world's hunger problem. He just wants us to be ourselves. You know what else? More often than not, he wants to talk back to us. Not just through the Bible and other people, but also straight to our hearts. He loves to remind us how much he cares for us, especially during the toughest moments of our day.

Why not take a few minutes right now to just close your eyes and talk with God. You can even use your phone if you want. Tell him how you're feeling and what's weighing heavily on your mind. Then spend some time just listening to what he's saying back. You don't have to worry about wasting any phone charge if there's a long pause. And heaven's always got full network coverage.

God's mind

Pray in the Spirit at all times. Pray with all kinds of prayers, and ask for everything you need. To do this you must always be ready. Never give up. Always pray for all of God's people.

(Ephesians 6:18)

Never stop praying.

(1 Thessalonians 5:17)

'When you pray, don't be like the hypocrites. They love to stand in the synagogues and on the street corners and pray loudly. They want people to see them. The truth is, that's all the reward they will get. But when you pray, you should go into your room and close the door. Then pray to your Father. He is there in that private place. He can see what is done in private, and he will reward you. And when you pray, don't be like the people who don't know God. They say the same things again and again. They think that if they say it enough, their god will hear them. Don't be like them. Your Father knows what you need before you ask him. So this is how you should pray: "Our Father in heaven, we pray that your name will always be kept holy. We pray that your kingdom will come – that what you want will be done here on earth, the same as in heaven. Give us the food we need for today. Forgive our sins, just as we have forgiven those who did wrong to us. Don't let us be tempted, but save us from the Evil One."'

(Matthew 6:5–13)

Anyone who lives the way God wants can pray, and great things will happen.

(James 5:16b)

Your thoughts are beyond my understanding. They cannot be measured!

(Psalm 139:17)

Your mind

- **What's the longest I've ever prayed?**

....

- **What's the longest I've ever gone without praying?**

....

- **What do I feel like when I've neglected talking to God?**

....

- **How do I know God is listening to me and answering my prayers?**

....

- **What are four things I can pray for right now?**

1. ....

2. ....

3. ....

4. ....

- **Now do it!**

Chip Kendall, *The Mind of chipK: Enter at Your Own Risk*, Authentic Media, 2005

Reaction Reaction Reaction Reaction

CIRCLE:

TICK:

Total rubbish ☐   Not sure ☐   Worth thinking about ☐   Genius ☐

FILL:

....

....

Name: Lydia Pugh

Age: 16

Town: Andover

Schools subjects: Drama, R.E.

Musical instrument you'd like to play if any?

Drums or piano. That would be quite cool.

Best song ever written?

'Voice of Truth' by Casting Crowns. Definitely.

What do you look for in a man?

Humour!

Do you pray?

Yes. A lot.

What would you say to someone who wants to pray but they don't know how?

Just sit and talk to God and say whatever you want, then say 'Amen' at the end.

Does God ever talk back to you?

Yeah. His response usually depends on what I ask. Usually it's 'Yes' or 'Wait'.

Are there ever any incorrect prayers to pray?

No. Unless they're really weird and horrible like, 'Please kill this person!'

Wake Up and Pray

I want to encourage you to pray more. If that statement makes you want to stop reading then maybe you need to read this more than anyone. If I'm honest, I rarely pray for the bigger picture. I pray for my family and for my personal concerns but I rarely, if ever, pray for the plight of other countries and situations, such as Iraq or Syria, or for the poverty stricken people caught up in earthquakes or floods. Somehow I forget, which must actually mean I don't care very much.

R ecently I had a conversation with a friend whose husband is an Iraqi living in the UK. His family, brothers, uncles, aunts and cousins (all 62 of them), are still in Iraq. He lives every day with the fear that any one of them could be killed. Hearing my friend speak of life in Baghdad and the fear that constantly follows everyone there, and the hundred innocents brought dead into hospitals every day, made me want to pray. **IT MADE ME WANT TO GET DOWN ON MY KNEES AND REALLY PRAY**. For God's mercy on the people living in Iraq, for God's justice in that situation and for his protection for innocent families trying to live their lives in peace.

The sad thing is that I've probably heard all those stories any time I switch on my TV, radio or computer, but I have chosen not to really hear them. When I see those stories on the news: bombs in market places, women wailing, men shouting, I usually switch channels. It's too much to take in, so I switch off because I don't want to deal with what I am seeing.

I know it is impossible to personally make right all the wrongs in this crazy world. But I also know that as a Christian I am called to love others as I love myself and to look after the poor and persecuted and to weep with those who weep. For me, one conversation with someone who has family members in Iraq has had more impact than all the bloodstained images I've seen on the *Six O'Clock News*. Why? Because it was one story; it was manageable. It has made me pray.

I'm not just telling you all this to get you to pray for Iraq, for Syria, or for the other tragic situations around the world. I'm challenging you to get yourself to a place where you want to. Get yourself to a place where you care. Do whatever it takes to wake up, slap your own face and think about others. Whether it's watching the news, doing some research, imagining your city as a war zone or whatever works for you. Find something that can stop you in your tracks to pray. The tragedies in the world are too big for us to understand or fix but if we can pray then we can get someone involved who can.

ReactionReactionReactionReaction

CIRCLE:

TICK:

Total rubbish ☐   Not sure ☐   Worth thinking about ☐   Genius ☐

FILL:

....

....

Hidden pearls

Our prayer life has changed over the years. When we were younger we prayed but not how we do now that we're old. We pray together every night, and pray for people by name. It helps us remind each other what we're thinking about. We even pray for our future great-grandchildren.

Praying for tea

A little while before I arrived on the scene, my parents were missionaries in France. Money was very tight for them during that time, and they lived a very streamlined life.

One day they got a call asking them if they could host a group of around twenty young people, who had been on mission just down the road, for tea. After a little prayer, my parents felt they should host the mission team, but had no money to go and buy the food. They continued to pray that God would help them to serve this group of young people.

The post came and went that morning with nothing helpful to the cause. My parents continued to pray, having no real idea of how they were going to provide tea for the group. Suddenly, there was a knock at the door. My dad opened it to find a special delivery postman standing there. He asked my dad to sign a sheet of paper, and then proceeded to count out notes of cash into his hand. **IT WAS JUST ENOUGH TO GO AND BUY THE FOOD NEEDED FOR THE MISSION TEAM!**

As it turned out, a young person my parents had worked with in France had been praying, and felt that God had told him to send my parents some money. However, he felt very specifically that it should be cash, and that he should use the special cash delivery service that the French post office offered at the time. If he had sent a cheque, used the normal postal service, or waited even a day on the instructions God had given him, the money wouldn't have helped my parents in that situation.

My parents believed that if they were faithful in prayer, God would faithfully provide for their need. The young man who sent them the money believed that if he faithfully prayed, God would faithfully lead him in his actions. God used the faithful prayers of his people to bring about his purposes.

Do you prioritize prayer in your daily life, believing that God listens and can powerfully work in any situation, even by using you as the answer to someone's prayer?

Read Philippians 4:6–7. See also Psalm 25, Luke 18:1–8, John 15:7.

Reflect

- *What do the verses from Philippians 4 and the prayerful song of Psalm 25 teach you about prayer?*

- *What do you think Jesus is saying through the parable of the persistent widow, in Luke 18, about our attitude to prayer and God's response?*

Respond

- *Pray in faith that God listens and responds to prayer. For every minute that you spend praying for your need, spend the same amount of time listening to see how God may be calling you to be the answer to other people's prayers.*

Remember

- *Pray faithfully in all things and see how your faithful Father God responds.*

ReactionReactionReactionReaction

CIRCLE:

TICK:
Total rubbish ☐   Not sure ☐   Worth thinking about ☐   Genius ☐

FILL:

....

....

....

....

BREAD

Fast food – McDonald's, Burger King, KFC – walk in, order, eat, burp – all over in minutes. But homemade bread is not made quickly.

Imagine sitting in a warm kitchen, feeling hungry, watching someone making bread . . . measuring flour, mixing yeast, sugar and water, making the dough, kneading it . . .

The dough is put in a bowl and left to rise – a warm, yeasty smell fills the kitchen. Your hunger grows just thinking about the crusty, fresh bread to come.

BUT YOU HAVE TO WAIT . . .

More kneading and shaping. Placed in the loaf tin, the dough looks closer to fulfilling its potential – but it's left to rise once more.

AND YOU HAVE TO WAIT . . .

Into the oven, another wait, more intense smells, growing hunger, a temptation to eat anything – but no, you'll wait for crusty, fresh bread . . .

Finally the bread is ready. And you have to wait for it to cool . . .

Are you hungry for God? Are you waiting for God to answer your prayer, to satisfy your need?

Perhaps, like homemade bread, God cannot be rushed. Perhaps, like yeast silently breathing and growing, something is happening unseen. **PERHAPS YOU NEED TO WAIT A LITTLE LONGER.**

Take some dough and knead it in your hands. Breathe in the warm, yeasty smell. Think about what it could become. Tell God about your hunger – ask God to satisfy your need. Tell God about your unanswered prayers, about what it's like to wait.

David despaired that God would ever answer his prayer and come and help him. He felt abandoned and alone. **Read Psalm 13** – and see how it ends.

David affirms his trust in God, in spite of still waiting. He decides to trust and chooses to thank God in spite of feeling so desolate. Can you? Eat some bread as a way of saying that you will trust God to satisfy your hunger and to answer your prayer.

Jenny Baker, *Transforming Prayer*, Spring Harvest Publishing and Authentic Media, 2004

Reaction Reaction Reaction Reaction

CIRCLE:

TICK:

Total rubbish ☐   Not sure ☐   Worth thinking about ☐   Genius ☐

FILL:

....

....

....

....

Get out as many old photo albums as you can find, and browse through them for a while. Enjoy the memories of the relationships represented there.

Now **read Colossians 1:7–14**

WHO HAVE YOU LEARNED THE TRUTH FROM? Perhaps using the photos as a memory jogger, make a list of the key individuals in your life who have influenced you by their words and deeds. Beside their name, detail what their major impact was – perhaps it was simply one statement or their strength in a particular area. These people may not even be folks that you know well. It could be someone you once heard speak at an event or whose story inspired you.

NOW LET THEM KNOW. I had the privilege of connecting two people last year, where a young girl owed her escape from a shocking lifestyle to a youth worker friend of mine. The youth worker had moved away before this girl had got it together enough to say thanks, but a random meeting and two emails later, something very beautiful had happened. It may take some effort to track people down but web searches make this a much easier task than it used to be. You will be amazed how encouraged people will be by what you tell them. Sometimes it is all the more special because there has been a substantial time lag.

On another tack, who prays for you? You may be surprised how many people do pray for you. Usually once folks have connected with you in a significant way, you stay in their hearts and minds, as with Paul and the Colossians in the passage. Is there a group of people that you regularly share information about your life with? If not, assemble an email, text or physical group who can regularly pray for you. Remember prayer is not only for negative situations. So often we only employ the might of God's people on their knees when we are in crisis mode. We miss out on the blessings and impact that may come when we also invite people to pray into our joys and successful areas, for the deepening and widening of our gifts or for ears to hear the Spirit's prompting in life situations. This anomaly also feeds our false belief that, in the successful times, we are achieving what we achieve through our own efforts.

Our housegroup has a 'prayer chain', whereby a prayer request is texted to the next person in the loop, who then passes it on. All I need to remember is which person is after me in the loop and twelve people are praying on the issue within a very short space of time. I have resolved to make sure that I send as many 'offensive' requests as 'defensive' requests, so we will be on the attack in our prayers and not just fire-fighting.

Sort out who your sisters and brothers in arms will be.

Andy Flannagan, *God 360°*, Spring Harvest Publishing and Authentic Media, 2006

ReactionReactionReactionReaction

CIRCLE:

TICK:

Total rubbish ☐   Not sure ☐   Worth thinking about ☐   Genius ☐

FILL:

....
....
....
....

FASTING

Fasting is perhaps one of the most neglected spiritual disciplines in our churches, although your experience may be different! Young people may have heard more about Muslims fasting during the month of Ramadan, or about the benefits of detoxing by fasting, or about David Blaine's 44-day fast in a Perspex box over the Thames, than they have about the tradition of fasting in the Christian church. And yet it is a practice found in all strands of the church throughout history. Today, some charismatic churches emphasize the role that fasting plays in spiritual warfare. The Anglican and Catholic churches encourage people to fast during Lent in some way. The Eastern Orthodox Church has four main periods of fasting, in addition to Wednesdays and Fridays being days of fasting. So it's there, just waiting to be rediscovered!

When you fast

Read Matthew 6:16–18

- Jesus says 'when' you fast – not 'if'
- Don't be hypocritical or a show-off
- If you do it to be seen by other people that's all the reward you'll get
- Giving, forgiving and fasting should be done secretly
- God will see you and reward you

Fasting was a normal part of Jewish life and Jesus wanted to make sure that they weren't doing it for the wrong reasons. Fasting is still emphasized in some parts of the church, but by and large it's not often talked about.

Fasting can be a way of controlling the things that control us. Instead of immediately rushing to satisfy our hunger for different things, it enables us to be more controlled and have a better sense of God's priorities. Fasting in the Bible was always about giving up food, and sometimes even drink – but you can also fast from anything that you feel is too important in your life.

Fasting guidelines

- Decide what to give up and how long to do it for

- Be realistic – start simply

- Stay healthy – going without drink for any length of time will make you ill. Get a doctor's advice if you are diabetic. You can always fast from something other than food, such as television or video games

- Decide how to use the time you free up – what will you pray for?

Jenny Baker, *Vibrant Spirituality*, **Spring Harvest Publishing and Authentic Media, 2004**

ReactionReactionReactionReaction

CIRCLE:

TICK:

Total rubbish ☐   Not sure ☐   Worth thinking about ☐   Genius ☐

FILL:

....
....
....
....

Break-fast

chipK's mind

I have a sort of special relationship with Kellogg's Crunchy Nut. Anyone who knows me well knows that I'm an obsessed lover of the stuff. I used it to illustrate a point once while preaching in a local church, and I found out afterwards that one of its inventors was right there in the congregation. I suppose it's a good thing I mentioned how much I enjoyed eating it!

T here are times (difficult times, I assure you), however, when I must refrain from eating, not just my beloved Crunchy Nut, but every kind of food, altogether. Instead, I spend the time I would normally spend eating, praying and reading the Bible. It's called 'fasting'. Whenever I'm in a situation where I desperately need to hear God's voice or see him accomplish something in my life, fasting is my way of saying, 'God, I'd rather hear from you than eat.'

People in the Bible did it all the time. Whenever the big prophet dude called a holy fast, the entire nation would spend a whole day just sitting there listening to him read from the Scriptures. Moses fasted when he went up on the mountain to talk to God and get the Ten Commandments. Jesus fasted for 40 whole days while he was tested in the wilderness. He went on to teach his disciples, saying, **'WHEN YOU FAST . . .' NOT 'IF YOU FAST'.** That means it's something everyone who's serious about being a follower of Jesus can and should do.

And once you've finished, I've got the ultimate 'break-fast' cereal . . .

God's mind

'When you fast, don't make yourselves look sad like the hypocrites. They put a look of suffering on their faces so that people will see they are fasting. The truth is, that's all the reward they will get. So when you fast, wash your face and make yourself look nice. Then no one will know you are fasting, except your Father, who is with you even in private. He can see what is done in private, and he will reward you.'

(Matthew 6:16–18)

'Do you think I want to see people punish their bodies on those days of fasting? Do you think I want people to look sad and bow their heads like dead plants? Do you think I want people to wear mourning clothes and sit in ashes to show their sadness? That is what you do on your days of fasting. Do you think that is what the LORD wants? I will tell you the kind of day I want: a day to set people free. I want a day when you take the burdens from others. I want a day when you set troubled people free and you take the burdens from their shoulders. I want you to share your food with the hungry. I want you to find the poor who don't have homes and bring them into your own homes. When you see people who have no clothes, give them your clothes! Don't hide from your relatives when they need help.'

(Isaiah 58:5–7)

Moses stayed there with the LORD for 40 days and 40 nights. Moses did not eat any food or drink any water. And he wrote the words of the agreement (the Ten Commandments) on the two stone tablets.

(Exodus 34:28)

Jesus ate nothing for 40 days and nights. After this, he was very hungry.

(Matthew 4:2)

Your mind

- **Why should I consider fasting?**

  ....

  ....

- **What else can I fast from besides food?**

  ....

  ....

- **Why is it best to fast in secret? (HINT: Matthew 6:18)**

  ....

  ....

- **When is the next time I will fast?**

  ....

  ....

Chip Kendall, *The Mind of chipK: Enter at Your Own Risk*, Authentic Media, 2005

ReactionReactionReactionReaction

CIRCLE:

TICK:

Total rubbish ☐   Not sure ☐   Worth thinking about ☐   Genius ☐

FILL:

....

....

....

....

Reality Check

PRAYER SPIDER CHART

When you start to pray it can sometimes feel a bit overwhelming because there are so many things you could pray for. Hopefully this Reality Check will help you organize your thoughts and split your praying into manageable chunks.

For this Reality Check you will need:

• A large piece of paper

• A pen

Instructions:

On a blank piece of paper draw a circle in the centre and write in it whatever is at the centre of your life. This might be your immediate family (write in their names), a good friend, or a girlfriend/boyfriend or something else.

Then draw lines out from the centre to more circles and write down other things that are important in your life. This can include things you are involved in or care about e.g. school, job, neighbours, friends, church, college.

From each smaller circle draw lines to circles containing more details about what you would like to pray about for these people or situations. For example, from the school circle you might add GCSE coursework, not getting into trouble, university places, making friends. From the friends circle you might add specific names or prayer requests.

Finally, think about any world situations or things that you are not directly involved in but would like to pray for and draw lines from the centre out to them. For example, the persecuted church, the political situation in the Middle East, child poverty. Make sure they are things you really care about or you won't pray for them.

You can add as many layers and as much detail as you want to the spider chart. It might look something like this:

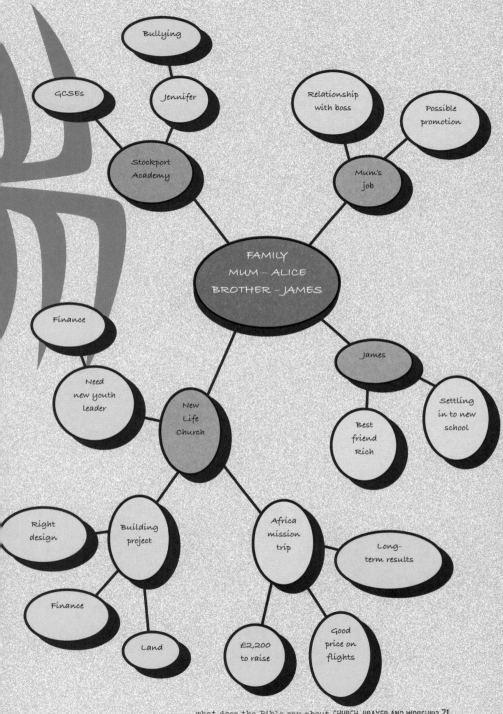

Worship

I will praise the LORD at all times. I will never stop
singing his praises. Humble people, listen and be happy,
while I boast about the LORD. Praise the LORD with me.
Let us honour his name.

(Psalm 34:1–3)

4

First up

What is worship? Is it the quiet singing bit at church? Is it a style of music involving guitar-led choruses? It would be quite easy to go through life thinking that worship was just those things. In fact worship is much more. Worship is a lifestyle, it's where you choose to praise and honour God in every circumstance and every situation. That might be by singing a little praise song as you skip along on a beautiful sunny day or it might be just continuing to put one foot in front of the other as you slog up a steep hill in life and not giving up.

When we were at college in California we had to be on the church dance team (to dance in worship) as part of our course. Our church believed in praising God with all your strength and the dancers would lead the movement in the same way the musicians led the singing. Of course some Sundays we would leap out of bed feeling full of life and absolutely love jumping around and praising God. Other Sundays, our bodies aching after spending all week in dance classes and rehearsals, feeling a bit homesick and with several assignments hanging over our heads, we certainly didn't feel like dancing. However, there was a very eccentric woman in charge of the dancers called Pam Chesboro and, no matter what, Pam did not let you out of dancing on a Sunday morning, regardless of how rough you felt. Obedience was the thing she drilled into us. You don't worship because you feel like it, you worship out of obedience to God, and in our case, obedience to our leaders. You worship God no matter how you feel. In all honesty, some of the best times of connecting with God happened for us on those days when we didn't feel like praising God but did it anyway. We once heard a story about a missionary gentleman whose wife died suddenly. He appeared in church the very next Sunday praising God as loudly as ever. Someone asked him, 'How can you praise God so passionately and cheerfully when your wife has just died?' He replied, 'Because God is still worth it!'

No matter what you are going through God is still worthy of your worship and praise, whether that involves singing, dancing, sweeping the floor or doing your homework with excellence. We hope this Life Lesson will give you a bit more of an insight into worship.

Worship

chipK's mind

If you were to ask me who my favourite Bible character is (apart from Jesus), I'd have to say David. He was described as, 'a man after God's own heart', anointed to do everything he attempted to accomplish. He killed giants in battle, married a princess, became a king himself, brought God's presence back to town and left behind a legacy of royalty, including the wisest man who ever lived, and eventually the Messiah. Wow, that's what I call a role model!

But probably David's most famous quality is that he was a true worshipper. He praised God on his harp during his humble beginnings as a lonely shepherd boy out in the fields with his father's sheep. He wrote loads of psalms documenting his escapes from Saul (his jealous, bloodthirsty predecessor), his victories in battle, and even his not-so-honourable moments (like needing to repent after sleeping with another man's wife). Eventually he set up a big tent where loads of musicians and worshippers could praise God at any time of the day or night. **DAVID'S PASSION WAS TO WORSHIP GOD, WHETHER HE FELT LIKE IT OR NOT.**

This should be the same for us today. A lot of the praise and worship songs we sing these days are positive and upbeat, and that's great. But really we should just as easily be able to come before God and honestly say, 'You know what? I've really messed up this week and I'm not even feeling very sorry about it right now either.' Jesus said that we should worship in spirit and in truth. When we start to open up and be honest with God, he can start to lovingly change us into the image of his perfect Son, Jesus. Like David, we too can be people after God's own heart.

God's mind

'But the time is coming when the true worshippers will worship the Father in spirit and truth. In fact, that time is now here. And these are the kind of people the Father wants to be his worshippers. God is spirit. So the people who worship him must worship in spirit and truth.'
(John 4:23–24)

So I beg you, brothers and sisters, because of the great mercy God has shown us, offer your lives as a living sacrifice to him – an offering that is only for God and pleasing to him. Considering what he has done, it is only right that you should worship him in this way.
(Romans 12:1)

I will praise the LORD at all times.
I will never stop singing his praises.
(Psalm 34:1)

Here are a few examples of brutally honest praise and worship:

LORD, why do you stay so far away? Why do you hide from people in times of trouble? The wicked are proud and make evil plans to hurt the poor, who are caught in their traps and made to suffer.
(Psalm 10:1–2)

LORD, I hate those who hate you. I hate those who are against you. I hate them completely! Your enemies are also my enemies. God, examine me and know my mind. Test me and know all my worries. Make sure that I am not going the wrong way. Lead me on the path that has always been right.
(Psalm 139:21–24)

Your mind

- **Who is my favourite Bible character?**

  ....

  ....

- **What's my favourite worship song?**

  ....

  ....

- **Which style of worship does God love best?**

  ROCK   CLASSICAL   HIP-HOP   DRUM 'N' BASS   COUNTRY
  JAZZ   R & B   METAL   OTHER ...

- **Why is it better to be honest than just sing nice songs?**

  ....

  ....

Chip Kendall, *The Mind of chipK: Enter at Your Own Risk*, Authentic Media, 2005

Reaction ReactionReactionReaction

CIRCLE:

😊 🙁 😐 😮 😌 😲

TICK:

Total rubbish ☐   Not sure ☐   Worth thinking about ☐   Genius ☐

FILL:

....

....

....

....

Name: *Sam Bolton*

Age: **15**

Town: **Birmingham**

Current Status: **Drummer**

What inspires you to play drums?

Any good drummers. I have friends who play drums, and they influence me to get better and they help me out a lot.

Do you feel that God helps you when you play?

Yeah, when we play worship songs I feel that he helps me not to mess up and to remember things (I tend to forget a lot).

Cleaning Fish

Chip talks

It had been nearly nine years since Charlie had last gone out fishing with his dad. It wasn't like they'd decided to never go fishing together again. Life just kind of took over – Charlie spent more time doing his own thing and his dad got more and more busy with his work. But now, after weeks of persuasion, Charlie's dad had convinced him to come.

While they were sitting there on the boat, Charlie and his dad were able to get re-acquainted with each other. In a lot of ways, the whole experience made Charlie feel like he was 10 years old again. After an hour or so, he was opening up and talking about some of his struggles – especially in terms of his walk with God. In all honesty, he felt he'd pushed God so far away and messed up so badly that he didn't think God was that interested in him any more.

Charlie's dad paused for a while before he finally responded: 'You know, you can't clean a fish before you catch it.' He went on to explain that **GOD DOESN'T EXPECT US TO 'CLEAN UP OUR ACT' BEFORE WE COME TO HIM. HE WANTS US TO APPROACH HIM JUST AS WE ARE** – after all, he knows everything there is to know about us anyway. He cares for us so much and designed us to need him, to crave him even, at the core of our existence. It's never too late to reconnect with our Heavenly Father, ask forgiveness and pick up where we left off.

This really made sense to Charlie, and he decided right there and then to make things right with God.

All of us are wired for worship. The question is – who (or what) are we worshipping?

What consumes our thoughts and energy the most in life? What do we spend most of our time and money on? Who can we not shut up about? Our boyfriend or girlfriend? Our favourite sport? Our wardrobe? Ourselves?

Jesus speaks to us in the middle of our craziness and simply says:

> 'Come to me all of you who are tired from the heavy burden you have been forced to carry. I will give you rest. Accept my teaching. Learn from me. I am gentle and humble in spirit. And you will be able to get some rest. Yes, the teaching that I ask you to accept is easy. The load I give you to carry is light.'

(Matthew 11:28–30)

Further reading: Matthew 6:25–34, Isaiah 1:18, Psalm 51, Psalm 139

ReactionReactionReactionReaction

CIRCLE:

😊 ☹️ 😐 😮 🙂 😲

TICK:

Total rubbish ☐   Not sure ☐   Worth thinking about ☐   Genius ☐

FILL:

....

....

....

Worship Kickin' Off

The gift of creativity gives us a way of reflecting on our walk with God – even if we don't see ourselves as particularly creative. We need to rediscover the creative arts. In such a materialistic society we tend to buy in all of our worship music rather than writing songs that reflect where we are as a local church. Maybe some of us have suffered tremendously and we need to have the opportunity to respond to God with laments like Jeremiah did. God wants us to worship him in freedom. Painting and sculpture, dance and drama – use the arts as expressions of worship to God. Just go wild and dance foolishly in worship!

D avid knew how to worship. In 2 Samuel he worshipped in wild abandonment when the ark returned to Jerusalem – he stripped and danced for the Lord. What makes it so amazing is that David was no child, he was king of one of the most powerful nations on earth. CAN YOU IMAGINE THE PRESIDENT OF THE USA PUBLICLY WORSHIPPING IN SUCH A FASHION?

If David was able to worship in such a way, what stops us from going crazy and allowing our praise to manifest itself in such ways? David's wife was pretty miffed when she saw him – embarrassed by the spectacle. Lives of worship affect those around – they cause reactions. Perhaps we are too afraid to worship in the liberty that God wants for us because of the fear of humiliation. Is this the source of our monochrome worship?

Worship is also about hungering for more of God. In his book *The God Chasers*, Tommy Tenney shares a great picture of God the Father. He tells a story of a young child trying to catch his father. The child keeps lunging to grasp the father but the father easily manoeuvres away each time. Eventually, the father's heart is touched. He sees how much the child wants to be with him and is overcome with a desire to be with the child. He swoops down, picks up and embraces the child.

As a child I know that I can never catch God. However, I capture his heart as I chase after him. He watches and sees how much I desire to be with him. I love that promise in Matthew that as we seek him, we will find him. He is obedient to that promise and meets with me. Our worship reflects our heart and our desire to be with him. How much do we seek after God in our worship?

Worshipping God is not about what he needs. It's about our relationship with him. It's about recognizing all that God deserves. And when we make time for him, when we put him first, he meets us. He's waiting for you now.

Andy Frost and Jo Wells, *Freestyle*, Authentic Media, 2005

Reaction Reaction Reaction Reaction

CIRCLE:

TICK:

Total rubbish ☐   Not sure ☐   Worth thinking about ☐   Genius ☐

FILL:

....

....

Hidden pearls

When we're not at church we worship God but we don't stand up and start singing with our hands in the air. You can just think of Jesus and you can feel that he's in your heart. You just talk to him don't you. I often say a little prayer in the car to Jesus. If you just think a prayer, he hears you.

Seaside

Helen talks

Let me tell you about this amazing festival in Norway called 'Seaside'. We performed at it loads of times with thebandwithnoname. After getting an early flight from Manchester we would arrive in Norway, jump into the minibus and find ourselves driving along these empty roads through amazing forests, passing cute little houses and perfect villages. The festival takes place on an island and the main stage is in this kind of natural amphitheatre in a clearing. Everyone sits out on the rocks or on the grass and watches the show; it's an amazing atmosphere. If you follow a short muddy path from the stage, you come to a little rocky beach where you can swim to the cliffs opposite, and if you are crazy like Chip you can jump off into the water from really high up!

At the end of each night, around midnight, they have a candlelit worship service up amongst the rocks, with hundreds of candles lit all over the place and people singing praise to God. When I'm there it's so easy to worship God – just thinking about it makes my skin tingle. What is it that makes worshipping there so easy? I wonder if it's because you are in the midst of one of the special parts of God's creation and it makes sense that in the midst of what he has made, it is easy to find him.

MOST OF THE TIME WHEN WE COME TO WORSHIP, WE ARE PRETTY FAR REMOVED FROM GOD'S NATURAL CREATION. I go to a big church in the city centre, which is amazing. I love the music, the lights, the energy, the fact that people are using their God-given creativity to worship him. But there is a different part of me that connects with God in the outdoors. When we get away from the stuff that we have created – the buildings, the noise, the cars – it's almost like we can get back to the world as God designed it.

It's in those wild places, at the top of mountains with the wind pounding your face or on beaches with the waves roaring, that you can see the hand of an all-powerful God. Or in those still, quiet moments where you watch a tiny insect going about its day that you see the intricacy of God's creation. Or in the rush of jumping off a cliff into the sea, or cycling down a mountain, that you can feel that adventurous spirit of God.

Do you sometimes struggle to connect with God in worship at church? We all encounter God in different ways. Why not try to get yourself out somewhere where you can begin to wonder at his creation, and start from there.

Read these verses to get started:

There are things about God that people cannot see – his eternal power and all that makes him God. But since the beginning of the world, those things have been easy for people to understand. They are made clear in what God has made.
(Romans 1:20)

Before the world began, the Word was there. The Word was with God, and the Word was God. He was there with God in the beginning. Everything was made through him, and nothing was made without him. In him there was life, and that life was a light for the people of the world.
(John 1:1–4)

'He alone made the skies, and he walks on the ocean waves. God made the Bear, Orion, and the Pleiades. He made the stars that cross the southern sky. He does things too marvellous for people to understand. He does too many miracles to count!'
(Job 9:8–10)

Reaction ReactionReactionReaction

CIRCLE:

TICK:
Total rubbish ☐   Not sure ☐   Worth thinking about ☐   Genius ☐

FILL:

....

....

Praise and Worship

Bible bit

Everything that breathes, praise the LORD. Praise the LORD!

(Psalm 150:6)

Shell's bit

When you 'worship' something, you show massive amounts of respect and admiration for that thing. You spend time thinking about it . . . you spend time talking about it . . . you simply love it!

Christians believe that God deserves to be worshipped more than anything else in the universe. That's why praise and worship should play a pretty big part in your life if you're a Christian. It's a way of communicating to God and saying 'thank you' for all the things he's done and expressing your passion and love for him. It's a way of saying, 'God, you mean everything to me and without you I am nothing.'

Now let me get one thing straight. It does not say in the Bible that the only way you can worship God is by singing along in front of a man with a guitar and a video projector! That is not necessarily worship if you're not doing it with the right attitude. Worship is an act of the heart. If you want to worship God by drawing pictures, then draw pictures. If you want to worship God by dancing, then dance. If you want to worship God by acting, then act. If you want to worship God by waving a flag above your head, then go for it! **YOU CAN WORSHIP GOD IN ANY WAY YOU WANT AND AT ANY TIME YOU WANT.** If you're someone who sings like a strangled alien but you want to worship God by singing, don't worry . . . just do it! God will love it because he doesn't care how it sounds. He just loves the fact that you are worshipping him! One thing God doesn't like very much is when you begin to worship something other than him. In the Bible it clearly says, 'You must not worship any other gods except me' (Exodus 20:3).

We can sometimes worship other things without even realizing it. Some people worship money. Some people worship other people or materialistic things such as cars, houses, clothes, etc. But how do you know if you're worshipping something else? Well, I was once told by a man called Winkie Pratney, that **YOUR GOD IS THE THING THAT YOU TALK ABOUT THE MOST,** that you spend most of your time thinking about, that you spend most of your money on, and that your life revolves around. I would really encourage you to make God your number one priority when it comes to worship. In fact, I would encourage you to make God your number one priority when it comes to everything. Let's worship the Creator and Giver of all things, not the things themselves.

Time to think and pray

How often do you worship God? Do you think you do it enough? Is God your number one priority or do you put other things before him! How do you enjoy worshipping God?

Shell Perris, *Something to Shout About Journal*, Authentic Media, 2007

ReactionReactionReactionReaction

CIRCLE:

TICK:

Total rubbish ☐   Not sure ☐   Worth thinking about ☐   Genius ☐

FILL:

....
....
....
....

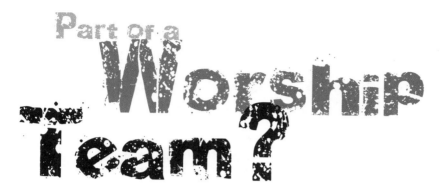

Part of a Worship team?

Chip talks

Did you know that even from the time of King David, God's people were led in worship by teams of musicians and singers? There were twenty-four shifts led by twenty-four different teams of Levites – one for each hour of the day – so that praise and worship was constantly being offered up from the Holy Tent. Can you imagine being given the 3 a.m. shift? Oosh! Well, at least all the yawning would make for a good vocal warm-up.

A re you part of a team that leads your church in praise and worship? If so, this extract has been written with you in mind. It's full of practical advice and tips for doing the best job you can. It's not exhaustive by any stretch of the imagination, but it's at least a good start.

Begin with thanks

In Psalm 100:4 we read, 'Come through the gates to his Temple giving thanks to him. Enter his courtyards with songs of praise. Honour him and bless his name.' Saying thanks to God is always a great way to start. It sets you up with a good attitude and promotes humility over expectation.

Know where you're going

My dad has been a worship leader for nearly forty years, and something he's always said is this: 'You can't lead someone somewhere you haven't already been.' It's important to spend quality time waiting on God in private worship before you step onto a stage to lead others into his presence. Then, once you know where you're going, you can honestly say, 'Taste and see that the Lord is good,' because you're speaking from personal experience. Psalm 34:8 says, 'Give the LORD a chance to show you how good he is. Great blessings belong to those who depend on him!'

Practise makes permanent

Whether you're a musician, vocalist, dancer or technician, this principle applies right across the board. Rehearsals make all the difference. Be ready for group rehearsals by going over and over the material on your own to start with. There is an anointing in preparation, and remember – the way you practise it will probably be the way you finally perform it, so make sure it's right from the beginning!

Always be on time

No excuses. This shows that you honour your leaders and respect your fellow team members. Being late only shows dishonour and disrespect. You may have to set your alarm earlier than you'd like, but it's always worth it. If it helps, just think of that poor Levite on the 3 a.m. shift!

It's all about the transitions

Sometimes we focus so much on learning and practising the songs themselves that we don't put much thought into the transitions between them. However these are equally important if we want the service to run as smoothly as possible, with minimal distractions. If there are key changes or tempo shifts involved, it may be worthwhile to include a prayer or encouragement to the congregation in order to bridge any awkward gaps.

Signals

Most worship leaders will use some sort of signals with their teams. These may be hand gestures to indicate they want to repeat a chorus or play more quietly, or even to end a song prematurely. It's important to be aware of which signals mean what. Quick, clear communication is essential.

Have fun

Remember that if you're smiling and being energetic, the people watching you are likely to follow suit. You've got so much to celebrate, so make it exciting!

You have shown me the way that leads to life. Being together with you will fill me with joy. Sitting beside you, I will never stop celebrating.

(Psalm 16:11)

Worship in the Christian Church

What are we going to do about this awesome, beautiful worship that God calls for? I would rather worship God than do any other thing I know of in all this wide world. I would not even attempt to tell you how many hymn books are piled up in my study. I cannot sing a note, but that is nobody's business. God thinks I am an opera star! God listens while I sing to him the old French hymns in translation, the old Latin hymns in translation. God listens while I sing the old Greek hymns from the Eastern church as well as the beautiful psalms done in metre and some of the simpler songs of Watts and Wesley and the rest.

I mean it when I say that I would rather worship God than do anything else. You may reply, 'If you worship God you do nothing else.'

But that only reveals that you have not done your homework. The beautiful part of worship is that it prepares you and enables you to zero in on the important things that must be done for God.

Listen to me! Practically every good deed done in the church of Christ all the way back to the apostle Paul was done by people blazing with the radiant worship of their God.

A survey of church history will prove that **IT WAS THOSE WHO WERE THE YEARNING WORSHIPPERS WHO ALSO BECAME THE GREAT WORKERS**. Those great saints whose hymns we so tenderly sing were active in their faith to the point that we must wonder how they ever did it all.

The great hospitals have grown out of the hearts of worshipping men. The mental institutions grew out of the hearts of Christian and compassionate men and women. We should say, too, that wherever the church has come out of her lethargy, rising from her sleep and into the tides of revival and spiritual renewal, always the worshippers were behind it.

We will be making a mistake if we just stand back and say, 'But if we give ourselves to worship, no one will do anything.'

On the contrary, if we give ourselves to God's call to worship, everyone will do more than he or she is doing now, only, what he or she does will have significance and meaning to it. It will have the quality of eternity in it – it will be gold, silver and precious stones, not wood, hay and stubble.

A.W. Tozer, *Whatever Happened to Worship?* Authentic Media, 2007

Reaction ReactionReactionReaction

CIRCLE:

TICK:

Total rubbish ☐   Not sure ☐   Worth thinking about ☐   Genius ☐

FILL:

....

....

....

....

Name: **Matthew Woodhams**

Age: **19**

Town: **North London**

Current status: **Student at Durham University**

What is your shoe size?

9 ½

How does God speak to you?

Sometimes he has spoken to me directly, but this is rare. Usually he speaks to me through the circumstances that I am in at the time.

Any examples?

Well, I wasn't sure whether I should be going to university this year, or deferring it to spend a year working for God. So I prayed about it, but didn't get a clear answer. I sent off an application to my university to ask if I could defer my place, and trusted God to give me the answer that he wanted. So my request was rejected, and I am now going to university in September, where I'm sure that God will use me for his purposes.

Pay to PRAISE

The story so far – David has sinned by putting trust in facts and figures over faith in God ... He has wasted time counting the number of men in his armies like a paranoid teenager playing Risk. He is given three options – three years' famine, three months' fleeing from enemies or three days' plague. What a choice! Without phoning a friend, David goes for option C but is appalled at the outcome, as Jerusalem is left on the point of annihilation. However, God is even more appalled and stops the angels of death at Araunah's house. He tells David to go and build an altar there to save his people.

Read 2 Samuel 24:18–25

I remember exactly where I was sitting when I first read verse 24. **'I WILL NOT OFFER BURNT OFFERINGS TO THE LORD MY GOD THAT COST ME NOTHING.'** I felt immediately convicted. How many of my 'offerings' of worship cost me very little at all? For most of us, if we're honest, there is not much sacrifice involved as we actually quite like singing songs and getting that warm fuzzy feeling that comes when people get together and share a common belief and purpose.

So I challenge you today to let your time with God cost you something. Perhaps to your comfort, perhaps to your schedule, perhaps to your self-respect or perhaps to your credibility. I often challenge those who are normally seated or standing motionless in worship to dance or move, and those who are normally busting their cool moves to be still and silent. Where you are, do something that costs, whether that means lying prostrate before God or singing within earshot of your neighbours. Other ideas to get you thinking could include reading your Bible in public (not necessarily out loud), leaving a whole evening free to simply worship, or visiting a church whose style of worship is very different to your own.

Andy Flannagan, *God 360°*, Spring Harvest Publishing and Authentic Media, 2006

Reaction ReactionReactionReaction

CIRCLE:

TICK:

Total rubbish ☐   Not sure ☐   Worth thinking about ☐   Genius ☐

FILL:

....
....
....
....

Reality Check

SCAVENGER WORSHIP

See how many of the items listed on the next page you can find in half an hour. Once you've finished your scavenger hunt, place the items you've collected in front of you and pick them up one by one. Make it an act of worship by contemplating how each item displays some aspect of God's nature, and then thank and praise him for who he is.

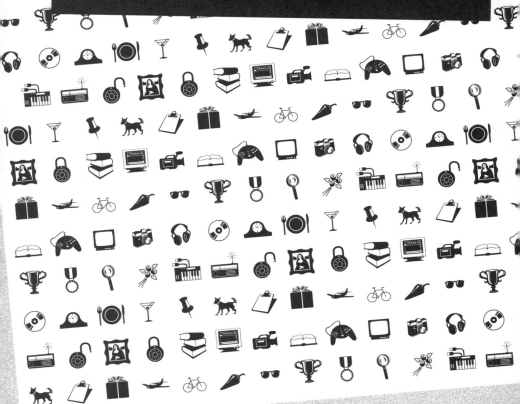

- ❏ rock
- ❏ clean sock
- ❏ CD
- ❏ piece of paper
- ❏ postcard
- ❏ plate
- ❏ paracetamol
- ❏ match
- ❏ picture
- ❏ coin
- ❏ chocolate
- ❏ hat
- ❏ glove
- ❏ soap
- ❏ battery
- ❏ salt shaker
- ❏ thimble
- ❏ trophy
- ❏ slug
- ❏ wallet

- ❏ leaf
- ❏ glass of water
- ❏ book
- ❏ plastic bag
- ❏ pencil
- ❏ candle
- ❏ sunglasses
- ❏ tablecloth
- ❏ balloon
- ❏ mirror
- ❏ key
- ❏ scissors
- ❏ bandage
- ❏ ring
- ❏ tea bag
- ❏ pepper grinder
- ❏ chapstick
- ❏ ball
- ❏ nail clippers
- ❏ bleach

- ❏ potato
- ❏ flower
- ❏ phone
- ❏ carrot
- ❏ paper clip
- ❏ jar of honey
- ❏ thorn
- ❏ shoe
- ❏ apple
- ❏ pen
- ❏ Blu-tac
- ❏ light bulb
- ❏ clock
- ❏ cuddly toy
- ❏ bottle opener
- ❏ pebble
- ❏ Post-it note
- ❏ rope
- ❏ badge
- ❏ onion

- ❏ dirty sock
- ❏ toilet roll
- ❏ cable
- ❏ box
- ❏ stamp
- ❏ magazine
- ❏ knife
- ❏ mug
- ❏ tissue
- ❏ lipstick
- ❏ scarf
- ❏ dictionary
- ❏ instrument
- ❏ TV remote
- ❏ cotton wool
- ❏ necklace
- ❏ slice of bread
- ❏ tape measure
- ❏ cross
- ❏ seed

Pray

Lord Jesus, thank you for your church. Thank you that I have an opportunity to be part of the most exciting movement in the world. Help me to be a useful part of your body, teach me to respect others and to use my gifts to help your body reach out to the world around me. Thank you for dying on the cross so that I can come to you directly in prayer and worship. Please help me to make the most of all the opportunities I have to talk to you – even when I'm in a crowded place! I pray that as I worship you I'll be able to lead by example so that others can know you as I have come to know you. Please wrap your loving arms around me and make me the person you want me to be. I give you all my dreams and desires – my heart is yours for the taking.

In Jesus' name,

Amen.